Prayer for Healing: Unfailing Prayers for Healing the Sick to the Holy Face of Jesus
by Simone Novelette

All Rights Reserved. No part of this publication may be reproduced in any form or by any means, including scanning, photocopying, or otherwise without prior written permission of the copyright holder. Copyright © 2015

Table of Contents

1. Do You Need A Healing Miracle?...3
2. "This Is My Body Which Will Be Given Up for You"...7
3. Veronica's Veil...11
4. The Main Prayers of The Devotion...19
5. The Keys to Success...33
6. Removing Unbelief and Fear...36
7. Removing Anxiety...48
8. Removing Depression...60
9. Speaking Positively...72
10. Intercessory Prayer...83
11. The Rosary, The Mass and Adoration...95
12. The Prayers of St. Therese to the Holy Face...98
13. Healing Scriptures..103
14. Holy Face Picture...109

1. Do You Need A Healing Miracle?

There are times when we have troubles that are so great, it seems there is no way out. Through our human eyes, we can see no possible way out of our dilemma. These are the times when we need a miracle.

Sickness can strike at any time, and it can seem as if we will never get well. Sometimes the doctors give up on us, but we can always rest assured that God hasn't. If the doctors can't seem to find the right solution to our problems, God can.

You may not be physically sick, but you may be ill emotionally. Emotional damage can be massive, and it can prevent you from functioning at optimal levels. If you are experiencing "emotional illness" and have tried to beat it unsuccessfully on your own, with medication or even with professional help, rest assured that even if all of this has failed, God can, and He will help you.

What if there was a guaranteed way for you to receive the healing miracle that you needed? What if this way of asking for a miracle was guaranteed by Jesus himself? All prayer is powerful. However, certain prayers contain a high level of efficacy. Throughout this book, I am going to take you on a journey that will change your life. You will realize more than ever the great love that Jesus has for you and mankind, you will feel more deeply connected to Jesus and the miracle you have been praying for will manifest in your life if you believe.

This is not my guarantee, it is the guarantee of the Lord Jesus himself who began this devotion. The origins of this devotion can be traced back to the day of Jesus' crucifixion. The devotion I speak of is the Holy Face devotion.

Throughout this book, I am going to give you a series of extremely powerful prayers. They will destroy the devil's attacks on your body and your life. These prayers will restore your body to the health and vitality that Jesus intended. You see, Jesus already bore the weight of your sickness on the cross. He already had his body broken, beaten, and surrendered to death for you. It is no accident that you are reading this book, it is divine providence. It is your time to take back your health from the hands of the enemy.

In the 1800s, the Holy Face devotion was carried out in the home of a wealthy lawyer named Leo DuPont and so many healing miracles occurred over the 30 years that he practiced this devotion, he was called "the greatest miracle worker in the history of the church". However, Leo DuPont never took credit for any of these miracles, he always gave the credit to the one whom it was due, the Lord Jesus.

To understand why devotion, the Holy Face of Jesus is so powerful and brings about so many healing miracles, it is necessary to journey back to the days leading up to the crucifixion of our Lord and also to take a closer look our Lord's passion.

2. "This is My Body Which Will Be Given Up for You"

In the Gospel of Luke, the Lord's Supper is recalled by the physician Luke in the twenty-second chapter from verses seven to twenty.

The Lord's Supper

*When the hour had come, He reclined at the table and the
apostles with Him. And He said to them, "I have earnestly
desired to eat this Passover with you before I suffer;
for I say to you, I shall never again eat it until it is fulfilled in
the kingdom of God."*

*And when He had taken a
cup and given thanks, He
said, "Take this and share it among
yourselves for I say to*

*you, I will not drink of the fruit of the vine
from now on until
the kingdom of God comes."*

*And when He had taken some bread and given thanks, He
broke and gave it to them saying, "This is My body which is
given for you; do this in remembrance of Me."*

*And in the same way, He took the cup
after they had eaten,
saying, "This cup which is poured out for you
is the new
covenant in My blood. (NIV)*

At the Passover, Jesus wanted to show his disciples using bread and wine, the power that resided in his body and blood. The institution of this ritual would eventually become a staple in the Christian church. The body and the blood of Jesus are ours, it is the sacrifice that He made for us. The entire body of Jesus is sacred, but in his face, all the pain of his passion both physical and emotional were registered.

The pain from the scourging that he received with every lash of that brutal whip which tore his flesh, the pain from the crown of thorns that tore and bore the flesh on his head. The pain of every nail that bore into his flesh and the humiliation of having the soldiers spit and punch him in the face. The exhaustion and the tiredness he felt from carrying the cross after losing so much blood from the scourging at the pillar.

Every feeling from each of these events was etched into his face. Think about it for a minute, doesn't our face display all that we feel, and if we wish to disguise those feelings, don't we usually have to make a conscious effort to do so? The face is the canvas for our emotions. Is it any wonder that all the pain and suffering that Jesus endured was so thoroughly etched on his face? Is it any wonder that by honoring his Holy Face which is a portrait of his anguish we can secure healing miracles?

3. Veronica's Veil

According to Catholic and orthodox tradition, a woman named Veronica met Jesus on the road to Calvary. She was so filled with compassion that she offered him a veil to wipe his face. Jesus was deeply moved by her compassion and rewarded her by leaving an image of his anguished face in the veil. Veronica eventually gave a relic of the veil to Clement who eventually became a bishop of Rome.

The relic is not the original veil, it is a replica of the veil that was touched to the original. There have been many claims that the original has been found, but these have yet to be verified as authentic. For three hundred years while the persecution of the church raged on, the relic of the veil was hidden in the catacombs. Once the persecution ceased, a church was built over the tomb of the apostle Peter, called the

Basilica of St. Peter. The veil has been kept in the church ever since.

The Revelations of Sister Mary of St. Peter

Between the years of 1843-1847, a Carmelite nun named Sister Marie began having a series of visions of Jesus in which she received revelations. During these revelations, Jesus told her that he would like to establish devotion to His Holy Face worldwide. The devotion would make reparation for the blasphemies that were being committed all over the world against his Holy name. The devotion would also be a way for everyone to appeal to his Father for whatever they needed. Jesus told Sister Mary that the devotion would be so powerful, it would be a means by which the devotee could solve any problem they faced and that the devotion would be enough to settle all the problems of their household. The devotion consisted of two major prayers which will be included in this book. They are "The Golden Arrow Prayer" and the "Litany to the Holy Face. Such a revelation and such a devotion would indeed be a blessing to humanity which is constantly beset by problems, but were Sister Marie's revelations real? Time and one miracle after another would prove that her visions were indeed very real.

The Glowing Veil

Sister Marie died in 1848, but not before she had told the bishop in Tours, France about her five years of revelations. She also had a friend named Leo Dupont who was a very wealthy lawyer with whom she also shared the details of the Holy Face devotion. In 1849, Pope Pius IX grew increasingly concerned about the Papal States due to an ongoing revolution that threatened to undermine the sovereignty of the church. He decreed that the faithful should offer public prayers in all the churches in Rome. As part of the appeal for God's mercy, a three-day exposition was held in which the relic of Veronica's veil was exposed in St. Peter's Basilica for the faithful to venerate it. On the third day of the showing, the veil began to glow. A soft light emanated from it and the face of Jesus on the relic became extremely distinct. The Pope ordered the bells in the Basilica to be rung and large crowds of people began to gather in the Basilica, and they all witnessed the miracle, for three hours the face of Jesus could be seen, and the light continued to emanate from the veil.

Artists began to capture the image on canvas and later these images were touched to the veil and sent out to the faithful in different parts of the world so that they could venerate it. This became a custom in the Vatican for many years. Leo Dupont with whom Sister Marie of St. Peter had shared her revelations and the prayers that she had received as part of it, obtained one of the Holy Face images and hung it in his parlor.

He along with his friends and visitors to his home began praying the Golden Arrow Prayer and the Litany of the Holy Face.

It wasn't long before miraculous healings began to take place among them and soon people all over Tours who suffered from all kinds of physical ailments would come and pray the prayers before the image of the Holy Face and they began receiving spontaneous healings.

More and more people began to come once news of the miracles spread, and the more they came and prayed the more they were healed. Mr. Dupont also kept a vigil light burning in a crystal lamp before the image and when the sick anointed themselves with it, many were healed. What is remarkable about the events that took place in Mr. Dupont's parlor is that it continued for thirty years until his death.'

Pope Pius was so impressed by the miracles, he declared that Mr. Dupont was one of the greatest miracle workers in the church. Mr. Dupont saw himself only as a vessel for the Lord's work.

In the same way that miracles were performed all those years ago through the Holy Face devotion, they are still being performed today. In Hebrews 13: 8 it says, "Jesus Christ is the same yesterday, today and forever!" YOU can receive your healing as well if you believe it!

The story of the Holy Face devotion does not end with Mr. Dupont because another nun named Sister Pierina who was born in 1900 and who died in 1945 also began to receive revelations from Jesus and his mother Mary. They asked her repeatedly to spread devotion to the Holy Face to make reparation for the insults Jesus suffered in the passion. These acts included the slaps and bunches he received in the face by the soldiers, the spits in the face he received, and the betrayal of Judas with a kiss.

During a vision, Sister Pierina was asked to have a medal struck with Jesus' Holy Face on it. On one side of the medal, she was to put Psalm 4:6 "May, O Lord, the light of Thy countenance shine upon us." On the opposite side she was to put the Host (consecrated bread) that represents Jesus' body, with the words, "Stay with us, O Lord." Luke 24:29.

Sister Pierina had very little funds to have the medal struck, but one day she found an envelope on her desk with the exact amount needed for the casting of the medal. Sister Pierina never found out who her benefactor was. Perhaps it was our Lord Jesus himself!

The first medal was offered to Pope Pius X11 and the devotion was made known to the church. During the Second World War, the medal became extremely popular and was worn around the neck by many soldiers. No soldier who wore the medal and was captured as a prisoner of war was ever executed.

Jesus told Sister Pierina, *"By My Holy Face you will obtain the conversion of numberless sinners. Nothing that you ask in making this offering will be refused you. According to the care you take in making reparation to My Face, disfigured by blasphemers, I will take care of yours, which has been disfigured by sin. I will reprint on it My image and render it as beautiful as it was on leaving the Baptismal font. I promise personal and spiritual protection to all who venerate this medal."*

If you would like to receive a medal you can get one at:
http://www.holyface.com/medals.htm

4. The Main Prayers of The Devotion

The main prayers of the devotion are, the *Golden Arrow Prayer* and the *Litany to the Holy Face.* The first prayer is called the golden arrow prayer because Sister Marie said that whenever this prayer was said she always saw a golden arrow of love pierce the sacred heart of Jesus. The second part of the devotion is the litany of the Holy Face which pays homage to Jesus' face by recalling his life from birth, death, and resurrection. The prayers are best said before an image of the Holy Face.

Each prayer in this devotion should be said with confidence as you gaze upon the face of the Lord. Our Lord told Sister Pierina that those who gaze on his Holy Face bring him great consolation. When you have finished saying both the Golden Arrow Prayer and the Litany, then you should offer up the Holy Face of Jesus to the Eternal Father for your healing.

A picture of the Holy Face will be included at the end of this book and it can be printed out for your personal use or if you would prefer a canvas version that you can place on your wall. It can be ordered at shop.thecatholicwomansvoice.com.

Jesus also made some promises to Sister Marie of St. Peter about those who would faithfully practice this devotion, these are listed below:

1. All those who honor My Face in a spirit of reparation will by so doing perform the office of the pious Veronica. According to the care they take in making reparation to My Face, disfigured by blasphemers, so will I take care of their souls which have been disfigured by sin. My Face is the seal of the

Divinity, which has the virtue of reproducing in souls the image of God.

2. Those who by words, prayers, or writing defend My cause in this work of reparation I will defend before My Father and will give them My kingdom.

3. By offering My Face to My Eternal Father, nothing will be refused, and the conversion of many sinners will be obtained.

4. By My Holy Face, they will work wonders, appease the anger of God, and draw down mercy on sinners.

5. As in a kingdom, they can procure all that is desired with a coin stamped with the King's effigy, so in the Kingdom of Heaven, they will obtain all they desire with the precious coin of My Holy Face.

6. Those who on earth contemplate the wounds of My Face shall in Heaven behold it radiant with glory.

7. They will receive in their souls a bright and constant irradiation of My Divinity, that by their likeness to My Face they shall shine with particular splendor in Heaven.

8. I will defend them, I will preserve them, and I assure them of final perseverance.

THE "GOLDEN ARROW" PRAYER

May the most holy, most sacred, most adorable, most incomprehensible and unutterable Name of God be always praised, blessed, loved, adored and glorified, in Heaven, on earth, and under the earth, by all the creatures of God, and by the Sacred Heart of Our Lord Jesus Christ in the Most Holy Sacrament of the Altar.

Amen.

LITANY TO THE HOLY FACE

Lord, have mercy on us.
Christ, have mercy on us.

Lord, have mercy on us.
Christ, hear us.
Christ, graciously hear us.
Holy Virgin Mary, pray for us.

O adorable Face, which was adored with profound respect by Mary and Joseph when they saw Thee for the first time, have mercy on us.

O adorable Face, which in the Stable of Bethlehem didst ravish with joy the angels, the shepherds and the Magi, have mercy on us.

O adorable Face, which in the Temple didst transpierce with a dart of love the saintly old man Simeon and the prophetess Anna, have mercy on us.

O adorable Face, which was bathed in tears in Thy holy infancy, have mercy on us
O adorable Face, which, when Thou didst appear in the Temple at twelve years of age, didst fill with admiration the Doctors of the law, have mercy on us.

O adorable Face, white with purity and ruddy with charity, have mercy on us.
O adorable Face, more beautiful than the sun, more lovely than the moon, more brilliant than the stars, have mercy on us.

O adorable Face, fresher than the roses of spring, have mercy on us.
O adorable Face, more precious than gold, silver, and diamonds have mercy on us.
O adorable Face, whose charms are so ravishing, and whose grace is so attractive, have mercy on us.

O adorable Face, whose every feature is characterized by nobility,
O adorable Face, contemplated by angels, have mercy on us.

O adorable Face, sweet delectation of the Saints, have mercy on us
O adorable Face, masterpiece of the Holy Ghost, in which the Eternal Father is well pleased, have mercy on us.

O adorable Face, delight of Mary and Joseph, have mercy on us.
O adorable Face, ineffable mirror of the Divine perfections, have mercy on us.
O adorable Face, whose beauty is always ancient and always new, have mercy on us.

O adorable Face, which appeases the wrath of God, have mercy on us.
O adorable Face, which makes the devils tremble, have mercy on us.
O adorable Face, treasure of graces and of blessings, have mercy on us.
O adorable Face, exposed in the desert to the inclemency of the weather, have mercy on us.
O adorable Face, scorched with the heat of the sun and bathed with sweat in Thy journeys, O adorable Face, whose expression is all divine, have mercy on us.

O adorable Face, whose modesty and
sweetness attracted both the just and sinners,
have mercy on us.

O adorable Face, which gave a holy kiss to
the little children, after having blessed them,
have mercy on us.

O adorable Face, troubled and weeping at
the tomb of Lazarus, have mercy on us.

O adorable Face, brilliant as the sun, and
radiant with glory on the Mountain of Tabor,
have mercy on us.

O adorable Face, sorrowful at the sight of
Jerusalem, and shedding tears on that
ungrateful city, have mercy on us.

O adorable Face, bowed down to the earth,
in the Garden of Olives, and covered with
confusion for our sins, have mercy on us.

O adorable Face, bathed in a bloody sweat, have mercy on us.

O adorable Face, kissed by the traitor Judas, have mercy on us.

O adorable Face, whose sanctity and majesty smote the soldiers with fear and cast them to the ground, have mercy on us.

O adorable Face, struck by a vile servant, shamefully blindfolded, and profaned by the sacrilegious hands of Thine enemies, have mercy on us.

O adorable Face, defiled with spittle, and bruised by innumerable buffets and blows, have mercy on us.

O adorable Face, whose Divine look wounded the heart of Peter, with a dart of sorrow and love, have mercy on us.

O adorable Face, humbled for us at the tribunals of Jerusalem, have mercy on us.
O adorable Face, which didst preserve Thy serenity when Pilate pronounced the fatal sentence, have mercy on us.

O adorable Face, covered with sweat and blood, and falling in the mire under the heavy weight of the Cross, have mercy on us.

O adorable Face, worthy of all our respect, veneration and worship, have mercy on us.

O adorable Face, wiped with a veil by a pious woman on the road to Calvary, have mercy on us.

O adorable Face, raised on the instrument of most shameful punishment, have mercy on us.

O adorable Face, whose brow was covered with Thorns, have mercy on us.

O adorable Face, whose eyes were filled with tears of blood, have mercy on us.

O adorable Face, into whose mouth was poured gall and vinegar, have mercy on us.

O adorable Face, whose hair and beard were plucked out by the executioners, have mercy on us.

O adorable Face, which was made like to that of a leper, have mercy on us.

O adorable Face, whose incomparable beauty was obscured under the dreadful cloud of the sins of the world, have mercy on us.

O adorable Face, covered with the sad shades of death, have mercy on us.

O adorable Face, washed and anointed by Mary and the holy women and wrapped in a shroud, have mercy on us.

O adorable Face, enclosed in the sepulcher, have mercy on us.

O adorable Face, all resplendent with glory and beauty on the day of the Resurrection, have mercy on us.

O adorable Face, all dazzling with light at the moment of Thy Ascension, have mercy on us.
O adorable Face, hidden in the Eucharist, have mercy on us.

O adorable Face, which will appear at the end of time, in the clouds, with great power and great majesty, have mercy on us.

O adorable Face, which will cause sinners to tremble, have mercy on us.

O adorable Face, which will fill the just with joy for all eternity, have mercy on us.

Lamb of God, who takes away the sins of the world, spare us, O Lord

Lamb of God, who takes away the sins of the world, graciously hear us, O Lord.

Lamb of God, who takes away the sins of the world, have mercy on us.

5. The Keys to Success

I believe that the reason the Holy Face Devotion is so powerful is because it incorporates praise and adoration. This is the same reason why adoration of the blessed sacrament is also powerful.

It says in the Bible that the Lord inhabits the praises of his people.

Adoration of the Holy Face brings such miracles because it glorifies the agony and passion of Jesus.

Physical and emotional healing will be yours as you begin to adore and praise Jesus through his Holy Face and then ask for what you need.

Be specific with your prayers for emotional and physical healing, speak to your specific pain in your prayers, and ask for them to be removed in the name of Jesus.

You need to be specific about the miracles and problems you want to be removed because there are often evil spirits causing obstacles through demonic attachments and they must be named. In other words, they must be "called out to be removed.".

Think about it, if you are inside a house and someone comes calling outside if they do not specifically call your name, would you come out?

Pray the devotion and apply the blood of Jesus. Call out your infirmities by name and bind them in the name of Jesus. You have authority in the name of Jesus even as a layperson. Call on the Eternal Father and remind him of his son's agony to secure your victory!

What is your pain?

Take a look at the Holy Face of Jesus', do you realize that he has already absorbed that pain.

There is a picture at the end of this book of the Holy Face of Jesus.

Look on that face, He has already borne your agony. Claim your healing because the devil is defeated. The Bible says that is for freedom that Christ has set us free. (Galatians 5:1)

Jesus' agony should not be in vain. He paid the price to set us free from emotional pain and physical infirmities.

However, sometimes He allows us to go through agonies so that He can mold us and be glorified. He also allows suffering because it pulls us closer to Him and when we overcome we have a testimony to inspire others.

6. Removing Unbelief and Fear

When we suffer from emotional and physical illness, sometimes our faith wavers and we start to ask God why it had to happen to us. We may begin to doubt that God is listening to our prayers or that he even cares. Doubt and fear often walk hand in hand, and they must both be eroded at the same time if you are to receive your victory.

PRAY THE "GOLDEN ARROW" PRAYER

May the most holy, most sacred, most adorable, most incomprehensible and unutterable Name of God be always praised, blessed, loved, adored and glorified, in Heaven, on earth, and under the earth, by all the creatures of God, and by the Sacred Heart of Our Lord Jesus Christ in the Most Holy Sacrament of the Altar. Amen.

PRAYER AGAINST FEAR AND DOUBT

Eternal Father, I offer up to you the Holy Face of your son Jesus Christ.
Turn away your eyes from my sin and look on his face.
I can do nothing without your assistance, and I ask that you destroy every shred of doubt and fear about my ability to get well.
Eternal Father, you have not given me a spirit of fear but of power, love, and a sound mind. (2 Timothy 1: 7)
I know that you have great plans for my life and that you want me to be in good health, heal this infirmity (<u>name it</u>) and destroy the very roots of it that have planted itself in my body/emotions. Look upon the face of your son Jesus as he advocates for my healing and turn your face away from my sins.
Eternal Father, I call to your remembrance his broken body and the blood he shed on Calvary and ask you to have MERCY on me.
AMEN

<u>Binding Prayer Against the Spirit of Fear</u>

Spirit of fear
I bring the cross of Jesus Christ and His Precious blood against you.
Through the intercession of the Blessed Virgin Mary,
St. Micheal the Archangel, St. Raphael the Archangel of healings, all the angels and saints.
I command you to leave me and go to the foot of the cross to receive your sentence.
In the name of the Father, Son, and Holy Spirit.
Amen

SAY THE LITANY TO THE HOLY FACE

Lord, have mercy on us.
Christ, have mercy on us.

Lord, have mercy on us.
Christ, hear us.
Christ, graciously hear us.

Holy Virgin Mary, pray for us.

O adorable Face, which was adored with profound respect by Mary and Joseph when they saw Thee for the first time, have mercy on us.

O adorable Face, which in the Stable of Bethlehem didst ravish with joy the angels, the shepherds and the Magi, have mercy on us.

O adorable Face, which in the Temple didst transpierce with a dart of love the saintly old man Simeon and the prophetess Anna, have mercy on us.

O adorable Face, which was bathed in tears in Thy holy infancy, have mercy on us
O adorable Face, which, when Thou didst appear in the Temple at twelve years of age, didst fill with admiration the Doctors of the law, have mercy on us.

O adorable Face, white with purity and ruddy with charity, have mercy on us.
O adorable Face, more beautiful than the sun, more lovely than the moon, more brilliant than the stars, have mercy on us.

O adorable Face, fresher than the roses of spring, have mercy on us.
O adorable Face, more precious than gold, silver, and diamonds have mercy on us.
O adorable Face, whose charms are so ravishing, and whose grace is so attractive, have mercy on us.

O adorable Face, whose every feature is characterized by nobility,
O adorable Face, contemplated by angels, have mercy on us.

O adorable Face, sweet delectation of the Saints, have mercy on us
O adorable Face, masterpiece of the Holy Ghost, in which the Eternal Father is well pleased, have mercy on us.

O adorable Face, delight of Mary and Joseph, have mercy on us.
O adorable Face, ineffable mirror of the Divine perfections, have mercy on us.
O adorable Face, whose beauty is always ancient and always new, have mercy on us.

O adorable Face, which appeases the wrath of God, have mercy on us.
O adorable Face, which makes the devils tremble, have mercy on us.
O adorable Face, treasure of graces and of blessings, have mercy on us.
O adorable Face, exposed in the desert to the inclemency of the weather, have mercy on us.
O adorable Face, scorched with the heat of the sun and bathed with sweat in Thy journeys, O adorable Face, whose expression is all divine, have mercy on us.

O adorable Face, whose modesty and sweetness attracted both the just and sinners, have mercy on us.

O adorable Face, which gave a holy kiss to the little children, after having blessed them, have mercy on us.

O adorable Face, troubled and weeping at the tomb of Lazarus, have mercy on us.

O adorable Face, brilliant as the sun, and radiant with glory on the Mountain of Tabor, have mercy on us.

O adorable Face, sorrowful at the sight of Jerusalem, and shedding tears on that ungrateful city, have mercy on us.

O adorable Face, bowed down to the earth, in the Garden of Olives, and covered with confusion for our sins, have mercy on us.

O adorable Face, bathed in a bloody sweat, have mercy on us.

O adorable Face, kissed by the traitor Judas, have mercy on us.

O adorable Face, whose sanctity and majesty smote the soldiers with fear and cast them to the ground, have mercy on us.

O adorable Face, struck by a vile servant, shamefully blindfolded, and profaned by the sacrilegious hands of Thine enemies, have mercy on us.

O adorable Face, defiled with spittle, and bruised by innumerable buffets and blows, have mercy on us.

O adorable Face, whose Divine look wounded the heart of Peter, with a dart of sorrow and love, have mercy on us.

O adorable Face, humbled for us at the tribunals of Jerusalem, have mercy on us.
O adorable Face, which didst preserve Thy serenity when Pilate pronounced the fatal sentence, have mercy on us.

O adorable Face, covered with sweat and blood, and falling in the mire under the heavy weight of the Cross, have mercy on us.

O adorable Face, worthy of all our respect, veneration and worship, have mercy on us.

O adorable Face, wiped with a veil by a pious woman on the road to Calvary, have mercy on us.

O adorable Face, raised on the instrument of most shameful punishment, have mercy on us.

O adorable Face, whose brow was covered with Thorns, have mercy on us.

O adorable Face, whose eyes were filled with tears of blood, have mercy on us.

O adorable Face, into whose mouth was poured gall and vinegar, have mercy on us.

O adorable Face, whose hair and beard were plucked out by the executioners, have mercy on us.

O adorable Face, which was made like to that of a leper, have mercy on us.

O adorable Face, whose incomparable beauty was obscured under the dreadful cloud of the sins of the world, have mercy on us.

O adorable Face, covered with the sad shades of death, have mercy on us.

O adorable Face, washed and anointed by Mary and the holy women and wrapped in a shroud, have mercy on us.

O adorable Face, enclosed in the sepulcher, have mercy on us.

O adorable Face, all resplendent with glory and beauty on the day of the Resurrection, have mercy on us.

O adorable Face, all dazzling with light at the moment of Thy Ascension, have mercy on us.
O adorable Face, hidden in the Eucharist, have mercy on us.

O adorable Face, which will appear at the end of time, in the clouds, with great power and great majesty, have mercy on us.

O adorable Face, which will cause sinners to tremble, have mercy on us.

O adorable Face, which will fill the just with joy for all eternity, have mercy on us.

Lamb of God, who takes away the sins of the world, spare us, O Lord

Lamb of God, who takes away the sins of the world, graciously hear us, O Lord.

Lamb of God, who takes away the sins of the world, have mercy on us.

7. Removing Anxiety

Anxiety comes from the enemy. Jesus asked that we be anxious about nothing and this includes our health.

If you are facing a difficult diagnosis or are in emotional turmoil, you may become anxious and your anxiety needs to be replaced with peace. Jesus is the author of peace. He can calm any storm. When we call down the peace of Christ in our lives the devil flees.

PRAY THE "GOLDEN ARROW" PRAYER

May the most holy, most sacred, most adorable, most incomprehensible and unutterable Name of God be always praised, blessed, loved, adored and glorified, in Heaven, on earth, and under the earth, by all the creatures of God, and by the Sacred

Heart of Our Lord Jesus Christ in the Most Holy Sacrament of the Altar. Amen.

PRAYER AGAINST ANXIETY

Eternal father, I offer up the Holy Face of your son and our
Lord Jesus Christ for the removal of every shred of anxiety about my health. Bind and destroy any evil forces that would try to bring any spirit of anxiety into my life. Cast out the spirit of anxiety and this infirmity (<u>name your illness</u>).
Look upon the face of your son as he advocates and pleads with you for my healing. Turn your gaze away from my sin and look instead on the face of your son in whom you are well pleased. (Matthew 17: 5) Look at the suffering on his face, which was made as a sacrifice for me and answer my prayer.

<u>Binding Prayer Against the Spirit of Anxiety</u>

Spirit of anxiety,
I bring the cross of Jesus Christ and His Precious blood against you.
Through the intercession of the Blessed Virgin Mary,
St. Micheal the Archangel, St. Raphael the Archangel of healings, all the angels and saints.
I command you to leave me and go to the foot of the cross to receive your sentence.
In the name of the Father, Son, and Holy Spirit.
Amen

SAY THE LITANY TO THE HOLY FACE

Lord, have mercy on us.
Christ, have mercy on us.

Lord, have mercy on us.
Christ, hear us.
Christ, graciously hear us.

Holy Virgin Mary, pray for us.

O adorable Face, which was adored with profound respect by Mary and Joseph when they saw Thee for the first time, have mercy on us.

O adorable Face, which in the Stable of Bethlehem didst ravish with joy the angels, the shepherds and the Magi, have mercy on us.

O adorable Face, which in the Temple didst transpierce with a dart of love the saintly old man Simeon and the prophetess Anna, have mercy on us.

O adorable Face, which was bathed in tears in Thy holy infancy, have mercy on us
O adorable Face, which, when Thou didst appear in the Temple at twelve years of age, didst fill with admiration the Doctors of the law, have mercy on us.

O adorable Face, white with purity and ruddy with charity, have mercy on us.
O adorable Face, more beautiful than the sun, more lovely than the moon, more brilliant than the stars, have mercy on us.

O adorable Face, fresher than the roses of spring, have mercy on us.
O adorable Face, more precious than gold, silver, and diamonds have mercy on us.
O adorable Face, whose charms are so ravishing, and whose grace is so attractive, have mercy on us.

O adorable Face, whose every feature is characterized by nobility,
O adorable Face, contemplated by angels, have mercy on us.

O adorable Face, sweet delectation of the Saints, have mercy on us
O adorable Face, masterpiece of the Holy Ghost, in which the Eternal Father is well pleased, have mercy on us.

O adorable Face, delight of Mary and Joseph, have mercy on us.
O adorable Face, ineffable mirror of the Divine perfections, have mercy on us.
O adorable Face, whose beauty is always ancient and always new, have mercy on us.

O adorable Face, which appeases the wrath of God, have mercy on us.
O adorable Face, which makes the devils tremble, have mercy on us.
O adorable Face, treasure of graces and of blessings, have mercy on us.
O adorable Face, exposed in the desert to the inclemency of the weather, have mercy on us.
O adorable Face, scorched with the heat of the sun and bathed with sweat in Thy journeys, O adorable Face, whose expression is all divine, have mercy on us.

O adorable Face, whose modesty and sweetness attracted both the just and sinners, have mercy on us.

O adorable Face, which gave a holy kiss to the little children, after having blessed them, have mercy on us.

O adorable Face, troubled and weeping at the tomb of Lazarus, have mercy on us.

O adorable Face, brilliant as the sun, and radiant with glory on the Mountain of Tabor, have mercy on us.

O adorable Face, sorrowful at the sight of Jerusalem, and shedding tears on that ungrateful city, have mercy on us.

O adorable Face, bowed down to the earth, in the Garden of Olives, and covered with confusion for our sins, have mercy on us.

O adorable Face, bathed in a bloody sweat, have mercy on us.

O adorable Face, kissed by the traitor Judas, have mercy on us.

O adorable Face, whose sanctity and majesty smote the soldiers with fear and cast them to the ground, have mercy on us.

O adorable Face, struck by a vile servant, shamefully blindfolded, and profaned by the sacrilegious hands of Thine enemies, have mercy on us.

O adorable Face, defiled with spittle, and bruised by innumerable buffets and blows, have mercy on us.

O adorable Face, whose Divine look wounded the heart of Peter, with a dart of sorrow and love, have mercy on us.

O adorable Face, humbled for us at the tribunals of Jerusalem, have mercy on us.
O adorable Face, which didst preserve Thy serenity when Pilate pronounced the fatal sentence, have mercy on us.

O adorable Face, covered with sweat and blood, and falling in the mire under the heavy weight of the Cross, have mercy on us.

O adorable Face, worthy of all our respect, veneration and worship, have mercy on us.

O adorable Face, wiped with a veil by a pious woman on the road to Calvary, have mercy on us.

O adorable Face, raised on the instrument of most shameful punishment, have mercy on us.

O adorable Face, whose brow was covered with Thorns, have mercy on us.

O adorable Face, whose eyes were filled with tears of blood, have mercy on us.

O adorable Face, into whose mouth was poured gall and vinegar, have mercy on us.

O adorable Face, whose hair and beard were plucked out by the executioners, have mercy on us.

O adorable Face, which was made like to that of a leper, have mercy on us.

O adorable Face, whose incomparable beauty was obscured under the dreadful cloud of the sins of the world, have mercy on us.

O adorable Face, covered with the sad shades of death, have mercy on us.

O adorable Face, washed and anointed by Mary and the holy women and wrapped in a shroud, have mercy on us.

O adorable Face, enclosed in the sepulcher, have mercy on us.

O adorable Face, all resplendent with glory and beauty on the day of the Resurrection, have mercy on us.

O adorable Face, all dazzling with light at the moment of Thy Ascension, have mercy on us.
O adorable Face, hidden in the Eucharist, have mercy on us.

O adorable Face, which will appear at the end of time, in the clouds, with great power and great majesty, have mercy on us.

O adorable Face, which will cause sinners to tremble, have mercy on us.

O adorable Face, which will fill the just with joy for all eternity, have mercy on us.

Lamb of God, who takes away the sins of the world, spare us, O Lord

Lamb of God, who takes away the sins of the world, graciously hear us, O Lord.

Lamb of God, who takes away the sins of the world, have mercy on us.

8. Removing Depression

Depression and illness often walk hand in hand. It is easy to focus on the size of the illness we are facing and lose sight of the bigness of God. God is capable of anything, for him, nothing is impossible (Luke 1:37)

Jesus rose Lazarus from the dead and went about curing all types of illnesses. He can certainly manage whatever you are facing if you trust in him.

PRAY THE "GOLDEN ARROW" PRAYER

May the most holy, most sacred, most adorable, most incomprehensible and unutterable Name of God be always praised, blessed, loved, adored and glorified, in Heaven, on earth, and under the earth, by all the creatures of God, and by the Sacred Heart of Our Lord Jesus Christ in the Most Holy Sacrament of the Altar. Amen.

PRAYER AGAINST DEPRESSION

Eternal Father, I offer up the Holy Face of your son and our
Lord Jesus Christ for the destruction of every spirit of depression that would attempt to penetrate my life. Remove and break the chains of my infirmity.

Eternal Father, I know that your wish for me is to have life and to have it abundantly (John 10: 10). Pull my joy from the hand of the enemy who has come to steal, kill, and destroy. Make me able to sing and make a joyful noise unto you. Eternal Father cast a glance on the anguished face of your son which was bruised for my iniquity. Listen to him as he pleads my case and have MERCY on me.

Amen

Binding Prayer Against the Spirit of Depression

Spirit of depression
I bring the cross of Jesus Christ and His Precious blood against you.
Through the intercession of the Blessed Virgin Mary,
St. Micheal the Archangel, St.Raphael the Archangel of healings, all the angels and saints.
I command you to leave me and go to the foot of the cross to receive your sentence.
In the name of the Father, Son, and Holy Spirit.
Amen

SAY THE LITANY TO THE HOLY FACE

Lord, have mercy on us.
Christ, have mercy on us.

Lord, have mercy on us.
Christ, hear us.

Christ, graciously hear us.
Holy Virgin Mary, pray for us.

O adorable Face, which was adored with profound respect by Mary and Joseph when they saw Thee for the first time, have mercy on us.

O adorable Face, which in the Stable of Bethlehem didst ravish with joy the angels, the shepherds and the Magi, have mercy on us.

O adorable Face, which in the Temple didst transpierce with a dart of love the saintly old man Simeon and the prophetess Anna, have mercy on us.

O adorable Face, which was bathed in tears in Thy holy infancy, have mercy on us
O adorable Face, which, when Thou didst appear in the Temple at twelve years of age, didst fill with admiration the Doctors of the law, have mercy on us.

O adorable Face, white with purity and ruddy with charity, have mercy on us.
O adorable Face, more beautiful than the sun, more lovely than the moon, more brilliant than the stars, have mercy on us.

O adorable Face, fresher than the roses of spring, have mercy on us.
O adorable Face, more precious than gold, silver, and diamonds have mercy on us.
O adorable Face, whose charms are so ravishing, and whose grace is so attractive, have mercy on us.

O adorable Face, whose every feature is characterized by nobility,
O adorable Face, contemplated by angels, have mercy on us.

O adorable Face, sweet delectation of the Saints, have mercy on us

O adorable Face, masterpiece of the Holy Ghost, in which the Eternal Father is well pleased, have mercy on us.

O adorable Face, delight of Mary and Joseph, have mercy on us.
O adorable Face, ineffable mirror of the Divine perfections, have mercy on us.
O adorable Face, whose beauty is always ancient and always new, have mercy on us.

O adorable Face, which appeases the wrath of God, have mercy on us.
O adorable Face, which makes the devils tremble, have mercy on us.
O adorable Face, treasure of graces and of blessings, have mercy on us.
O adorable Face, exposed in the desert to the inclemency of the weather, have mercy on us.
O adorable Face, scorched with the heat of the sun and bathed with sweat in Thy journeys, O adorable Face, whose expression is all divine, have mercy on us.

O adorable Face, whose modesty and sweetness attracted both the just and sinners, have mercy on us.

O adorable Face, which gave a holy kiss to the little children, after having blessed them, have mercy on us.

O adorable Face, troubled and weeping at the tomb of Lazarus, have mercy on us.

O adorable Face, brilliant as the sun, and radiant with glory on the Mountain of Tabor, have mercy on us.

O adorable Face, sorrowful at the sight of Jerusalem, and shedding tears on that ungrateful city, have mercy on us.

O adorable Face, bowed down to the earth, in the Garden of Olives, and covered with confusion for our sins, have mercy on us.

O adorable Face, bathed in a bloody sweat,
have mercy on us.

O adorable Face, kissed by the traitor Judas,
have mercy on us.

O adorable Face, whose sanctity and
majesty smote the soldiers with fear and cast
them to the ground, have mercy on us.

O adorable Face, struck by a vile servant,
shamefully blindfolded, and profaned by the
sacrilegious hands of Thine enemies, have
mercy on us.

O adorable Face, defiled with spittle, and
bruised by innumerable buffets and blows,
have mercy on us.

O adorable Face, whose Divine look
wounded the heart of Peter, with a dart of
sorrow and love, have mercy on us.

O adorable Face, humbled for us at the tribunals of Jerusalem, have mercy on us.
O adorable Face, which didst preserve Thy serenity when Pilate pronounced the fatal sentence, have mercy on us.

O adorable Face, covered with sweat and blood, and falling in the mire under the heavy weight of the Cross, have mercy on us.

O adorable Face, worthy of all our respect, veneration and worship, have mercy on us.

O adorable Face, wiped with a veil by a pious woman on the road to Calvary, have mercy on us.

O adorable Face, raised on the instrument of most shameful punishment, have mercy on us.

O adorable Face, whose brow was covered with Thorns, have mercy on us.

O adorable Face, whose eyes were filled with tears of blood, have mercy on us.

O adorable Face, into whose mouth was poured gall and vinegar, have mercy on us.

O adorable Face, whose hair and beard were plucked out by the executioners, have mercy on us.

O adorable Face, which was made like to that of a leper, have mercy on us.

O adorable Face, whose incomparable beauty was obscured under the dreadful cloud of the sins of the world, have mercy on us.

O adorable Face, covered with the sad shades of death, have mercy on us.

O adorable Face, washed and anointed by Mary and the holy women and wrapped in a shroud, have mercy on us.

O adorable Face, enclosed in the sepulcher, have mercy on us.

O adorable Face, all resplendent with glory and beauty on the day of the Resurrection, have mercy on us.

O adorable Face, all dazzling with light at the moment of Thy Ascension, have mercy on us.
O adorable Face, hidden in the Eucharist, have mercy on us.

O adorable Face, which will appear at the end of time, in the clouds, with great power and great majesty, have mercy on us.

O adorable Face, which will cause sinners to tremble, have mercy on us.

O adorable Face, which will fill the just with joy for all eternity, have mercy on us.

Lamb of God, who takes away the sins of the world, spare us, O Lord

Lamb of God, who takes away the sins of the world, graciously hear us, O Lord.

Lamb of God, who takes away the sins of the world, have mercy on us.

9. Speaking Positively

Sickness and emotional turmoil can make us feel negative about our lives and our circumstances. It is important that when we feel this way, we do not SPEAK negatively about life and our situation. We should always remember that life and death are in the power of the tongue. When we speak negatively about a situation, we unknowingly curse ourselves through personal negative confessions. This gives power to the enemy. Ask God to help you make your words positive at all times.

PRAY THE "GOLDEN ARROW" PRAYER

May the most holy, most sacred, most adorable, most incomprehensible and unutterable Name of God be always praised, blessed, loved, adored and glorified, in Heaven, on earth, and under the earth, by all the creatures of God, and by the Sacred

Heart of Our Lord Jesus Christ in the Most Holy Sacrament of the Altar. Amen.

PRAYER AGAINST NEGATIVE WORDS

Eternal Father, I offer up the Holy Face of your Son and our Lord Jesus Christ and ask you that bind every spirit of negativity that would give itself life through my words.

I ask you to cast these spirits back into the abyss from which they came. I know that reckless words pierce like a sword but the tongue of the wise brings healing (Proverbs 12: 18).

Help me, so that my tongue only always speaks wisdom and the truth of your love. I want your healing to permeate my life and my body.

Bless and keep me all the days of my life, look away from my sins and on the face of

your son, whose broken body and shed blood, have delivered me from death unto life.
Amen

SAY THE LITANY TO THE HOLY FACE

Lord, have mercy on us.
Christ, have mercy on us.

Lord, have mercy on us.
Christ, hear us.
Christ, graciously hear us.
Holy Virgin Mary, pray for us.

O adorable Face, which was adored with profound respect by Mary and Joseph when they saw Thee for the first time, have mercy on us.

O adorable Face, which in the Stable of Bethlehem didst ravish with joy the angels, the shepherds and the Magi, have mercy on us.

O adorable Face, which in the Temple didst transpierce with a dart of love the saintly old man Simeon and the prophetess Anna, have mercy on us.

O adorable Face, which was bathed in tears in Thy holy infancy, have mercy on us
O adorable Face, which, when Thou didst appear in the Temple at twelve years of age, didst fill with admiration the Doctors of the law, have mercy on us.

O adorable Face, white with purity and ruddy with charity, have mercy on us.
O adorable Face, more beautiful than the sun, more lovely than the moon, more brilliant than the stars, have mercy on us.

O adorable Face, fresher than the roses of spring, have mercy on us.

O adorable Face, more precious than gold, silver, and diamonds have mercy on us.
O adorable Face, whose charms are so ravishing, and whose grace is so attractive, have mercy on us.

O adorable Face, whose every feature is characterized by nobility,
O adorable Face, contemplated by angels, have mercy on us.

O adorable Face, sweet delectation of the Saints, have mercy on us
O adorable Face, masterpiece of the Holy Ghost, in which the Eternal Father is well pleased, have mercy on us.

O adorable Face, delight of Mary and Joseph, have mercy on us.
O adorable Face, ineffable mirror of the Divine perfections, have mercy on us.
O adorable Face, whose beauty is always ancient and always new, have mercy on us.

O adorable Face, which appeases the wrath of God, have mercy on us.
O adorable Face, which makes the devils tremble, have mercy on us.
O adorable Face, treasure of graces and of blessings, have mercy on us.
O adorable Face, exposed in the desert to the inclemency of the weather, have mercy on us.
O adorable Face, scorched with the heat of the sun and bathed with sweat in Thy journeys, O adorable Face, whose expression is all divine, have mercy on us.

O adorable Face, whose modesty and sweetness attracted both the just and sinners, have mercy on us.

O adorable Face, which gave a holy kiss to the little children, after having blessed them, have mercy on us.

O adorable Face, troubled and weeping at the tomb of Lazarus, have mercy on us.

O adorable Face, brilliant as the sun, and radiant with glory on the Mountain of Tabor, have mercy on us.

O adorable Face, sorrowful at the sight of Jerusalem, and shedding tears on that ungrateful city, have mercy on us.

O adorable Face, bowed down to the earth, in the Garden of Olives, and covered with confusion for our sins, have mercy on us.

O adorable Face, bathed in a bloody sweat, have mercy on us.

O adorable Face, kissed by the traitor Judas, have mercy on us.

O adorable Face, whose sanctity and majesty smote the soldiers with fear and cast them to the ground, have mercy on us.

O adorable Face, struck by a vile servant, shamefully blindfolded, and profaned by the sacrilegious hands of Thine enemies, have mercy on us.

O adorable Face, defiled with spittle, and bruised by innumerable buffets and blows, have mercy on us.

O adorable Face, whose Divine look wounded the heart of Peter, with a dart of sorrow and love, have mercy on us.

O adorable Face, humbled for us at the tribunals of Jerusalem, have mercy on us.
O adorable Face, which didst preserve Thy serenity when Pilate pronounced the fatal sentence, have mercy on us.

O adorable Face, covered with sweat and blood, and falling in the mire under the heavy weight of the Cross, have mercy on us.

O adorable Face, worthy of all our respect, veneration, and worship, have mercy on us.

O adorable Face, wiped with a veil by a pious woman on the road to Calvary, have mercy on us.

O adorable Face, raised on the instrument of most shameful punishment, have mercy on us.

O adorable Face, whose brow was covered with Thorns, have mercy on us.

O adorable Face, whose eyes were filled with tears of blood, have mercy on us.

O adorable Face, into whose mouth was poured gall and vinegar, have mercy on us.

O adorable Face, whose hair and beard were plucked out by the executioners, have mercy on us.

O adorable Face, which was made like to that of a leper, have mercy on us.

O adorable Face, whose incomparable beauty was obscured under the dreadful cloud of the sins of the world, have mercy on us.

O adorable Face, covered with the sad shades of death, have mercy on us.

O adorable Face, washed and anointed by Mary and the holy women and wrapped in a shroud, have mercy on us.

O adorable Face, enclosed in the sepulcher, have mercy on us.

O adorable Face, all resplendent with glory and beauty on the day of the Resurrection, have mercy on us.

O adorable Face, all dazzling with light at the moment of Thy Ascension, have mercy on us.
O adorable Face, hidden in the Eucharist, have mercy on us.

O adorable Face, which will appear at the end of time, in the clouds, with great power and great majesty, have mercy on us.

O adorable Face, which will cause sinners to tremble, have mercy on us.

O adorable Face, which will fill the just with joy for all eternity, have mercy on us.

Lamb of God, who takes away the sins of the world, spare us, O Lord

Lamb of God, who takes away the sins of the world, graciously hear us, O Lord.

Lamb of God, who takes away the sins of the world, have mercy on us.

10. Intercessory Prayer

There are times when we must stand in the gap for others and pray for them. It is in these times that we need to be more focused than ever on Jesus. Just as Jesus chose to take on the burden of our sins, in the same way, we must intercede for those around us who require spiritual help. Sickness and emotional pain are two of life's greatest challenges and if you can help someone to pray through it, then you are truly imitating Christ.

PRAY THE "GOLDEN ARROW" PRAYER

May the most holy, most sacred, most adorable, most incomprehensible and unutterable Name of God be always praised, blessed, loved, adored and glorified, in Heaven, on earth, and under the earth, by all the creatures of God, and by the Sacred

Heart of Our Lord Jesus Christ in the Most Holy Sacrament of the Altar. Amen.

INTERCESSORY PRAYER

Eternal Father, I offer up the Holy Face of your son and our
Lord Jesus Christ for the healing of (person's name). Remember Eternal Father that Jesus promised that by offering up his Holy Face to you we could settle all the affairs of our household.

I put complete trust in this promise as I offer up His Holy Face for the healing of (person's name).

Eternal Father lift (person's name) out of the hands of sickness/emotional pain.
Cast their illness back into the abyss from which it came.

Let (person's name) make a joyful noise to you continuously, go with (person's name) through the valley of the shadow of death.

Prepare a table before (person's name) and let (person's name) be a living testament to your healing power.

Eternal Father break the chains of disease and death/emotional pain as you look upon the face of your son, the one in whom you are well pleased.

Eternal father look, at His anguished face and His pleadings for the forgiveness of the sins of all mankind and have MERCY!

Amen

SAY THE LITANY TO THE HOLY FACE

Lord, have mercy on us.
Christ, have mercy on us.

Lord, have mercy on us.
Christ, hear us.
Christ, graciously hear us.
Holy Virgin Mary, pray for us.

O adorable Face, which was adored with profound respect by Mary and Joseph when they saw Thee for the first time, have mercy on us.

O adorable Face, which in the Stable of Bethlehem didst ravish with joy the angels, the shepherds and the Magi, have mercy on us.

O adorable Face, which in the Temple didst transpierce with a dart of love the saintly old man Simeon and the prophetess Anna, have mercy on us.

O adorable Face, which was bathed in tears in Thy holy infancy, have mercy on us

O adorable Face, which, when Thou didst appear in the Temple at twelve years of age, didst fill with admiration the Doctors of the law, have mercy on us.

O adorable Face, white with purity and ruddy with charity, have mercy on us.
O adorable Face, more beautiful than the sun, more lovely than the moon, more brilliant than the stars, have mercy on us.

O adorable Face, fresher than the roses of spring, have mercy on us.
O adorable Face, more precious than gold, silver, and diamonds have mercy on us.
O adorable Face, whose charms are so ravishing, and whose grace is so attractive, have mercy on us.

O adorable Face, whose every feature is characterized by nobility,
O adorable Face, contemplated by angels, have mercy on us.

O adorable Face, sweet delectation of the Saints, have mercy on us
O adorable Face, masterpiece of the Holy Ghost, in which the Eternal Father is well pleased, have mercy on us.

O adorable Face, delight of Mary and Joseph, have mercy on us.
O adorable Face, ineffable mirror of the Divine perfections, have mercy on us.
O adorable Face, whose beauty is always ancient and always new, have mercy on us.

O adorable Face, which appeases the wrath of God, have mercy on us.
O adorable Face, which makes the devils tremble, have mercy on us.
O adorable Face, treasure of graces and of blessings, have mercy on us.
O adorable Face, exposed in the desert to the inclemency of the weather, have mercy on us.
O adorable Face, scorched with the heat of the sun and bathed with sweat in Thy

journeys, O adorable Face, whose
expression is all divine, have mercy on us.

O adorable Face, whose modesty and
sweetness attracted both the just and sinners,
have mercy on us.

O adorable Face, which gave a holy kiss to
the little children, after having blessed them,
have mercy on us.

O adorable Face, troubled and weeping at
the tomb of Lazarus, have mercy on us.

O adorable Face, brilliant as the sun, and
radiant with glory on the Mountain of Tabor,
have mercy on us.

O adorable Face, sorrowful at the sight of
Jerusalem, and shedding tears on that
ungrateful city, have mercy on us.

O adorable Face, bowed down to the earth, in the Garden of Olives, and covered with confusion for our sins, have mercy on us.

O adorable Face, bathed in a bloody sweat, have mercy on us.

O adorable Face, kissed by the traitor Judas, have mercy on us.

O adorable Face, whose sanctity and majesty smote the soldiers with fear and cast them to the ground, have mercy on us.

O adorable Face, struck by a vile servant, shamefully blindfolded, and profaned by the sacrilegious hands of Thine enemies, have mercy on us.

O adorable Face, defiled with spittle, and bruised by innumerable buffets and blows, have mercy on us.

O adorable Face, whose Divine look wounded the heart of Peter, with a dart of sorrow and love, have mercy on us.

O adorable Face, humbled for us at the tribunals of Jerusalem, have mercy on us.
O adorable Face, which didst preserve Thy serenity when Pilate pronounced the fatal sentence, have mercy on us.

O adorable Face, covered with sweat and blood, and falling in the mire under the heavy weight of the Cross, have mercy on us.

O adorable Face, worthy of all our respect, veneration and worship, have mercy on us.

O adorable Face, wiped with a veil by a pious woman on the road to Calvary, have mercy on us.

O adorable Face, raised on the instrument of most shameful punishment, have mercy on us.

O adorable Face, whose brow was covered with Thorns, have mercy on us.

O adorable Face, whose eyes were filled with tears of blood, have mercy on us.

O adorable Face, into whose mouth was poured gall and vinegar, have mercy on us.

O adorable Face, whose hair and beard were plucked out by the executioners, have mercy on us.

O adorable Face, which was made like to that of a leper, have mercy on us.

O adorable Face, whose incomparable beauty was obscured under the dreadful cloud of the sins of the world, have mercy on us.

O adorable Face, covered with the sad shades of death, have mercy on us.

O adorable Face, washed and anointed by Mary and the holy women and wrapped in a shroud, have mercy on us.

O adorable Face, enclosed in the sepulcher, have mercy on us.

O adorable Face, all resplendent with glory and beauty on the day of the Resurrection, have mercy on us.

O adorable Face, all dazzling with light at the moment of Thy Ascension, have mercy on us.
O adorable Face, hidden in the Eucharist, have mercy on us.

O adorable Face, which will appear at the end of time, in the clouds, with great power and great majesty, have mercy on us.

O adorable Face, which will cause sinners to tremble, have mercy on us.

O adorable Face, which will fill the just with joy for all eternity, have mercy on us.

Lamb of God, who takes away the sins of the world, spare us, O Lord

Lamb of God, who takes away the sins of the world, graciously hear us, O Lord.

Lamb of God, who takes away the sins of the world, have mercy on us.

11. The Rosary, The Mass and Adoration

I could not write a book without touting what the wonderful St. Padre Pio referred to as "the weapon".

Are you praying the rosary?

If you are then you are already miles ahead of the devil. If you are not, you need to pick up one of the most powerful methods of warfare that we have in the world today.

This prayer makes the devil tremble. Father Amorth, who was once the chief exorcist for the Vatican, said that once during an exorcism he heard the devil lament about the power of this great prayer. The devil said that each "Hail Mary" was like a blow on his head and if Christians knew the power of the rosary he would be destroyed.

The rosary recalls the birth, death, and resurrection of Jesus, is it any wonder the devil hates this prayer. It is like a bad memory for him that won't go away. When you say it you are declaring his defeat.

The stories are endless about the miracles attained through the praying of the rosary. What I want you to do is to combine this devotion with the Holy Face devotion, the prayers, and binding prayers in this book.

This combination will explode the divine in your life and is sure to bring miracles! This is because you will now have the Blessed Mother at your side praying with you.

Father Amorth once said, "Anyone who goes to Mary and prays the rosary cannot be touched by Satan." He should know since he did battle with the devil in tens of thousands of exorcisms in his sixty years as a priest.

You need Our Lady for this battle and when you pray the rosary you are guaranteed of her presence. Finally, if you can go to daily mass then do so. It is the highest form of prayer the church has to offer.

If you can't go physically every day then go virtually, there are several live streams on YouTube daily. Spend time in adoration of the Blessed Sacrament as well. Again, if you can't go physically there are live streams on YouTube daily.

12. The Prayers of St. Therese to the Holy Face

The following prayers to the Holy Face were composed by St. Therese of Liseux, a Carmelite nun and doctor of the church who had a great devotion to the Holy Face. St. Therese is known as the "little flower". She believed that by doing small deeds of kindness we were doing "big" things for God. She had a great devotion to the Holy Face and composed many prayers about it. You can use them to further enhance your devotion as you pray for your healing.

O adorable face of Jesus,
sole beauty which ravishes my heart,
vouchsafe to impress on my soul
Your divine likeness
so that it may not be possible
for You to look at Your spouse
without beholding Yourself!
O my Beloved,
for love of You I am content
not to see here on earth

the sweetness of Your glance,
nor to feel the ineffable kiss
of Your sacred lips,
but I beg of You
to inflame me with Your love
so that it may consume me quickly
and that I (name) may behold
Your glorious countenance in heaven."

O Jesus, who in Thy bitter
Passion didst become
the most abject of men, a man of
sorrows", I venerate Thy Sacred Face
whereon there once did shine the
beauty and sweetness of the Godhead;
but now it has become for me as if it
were the face of a leper!

Nevertheless, under those disfigured
features, I recognize Thy infinite Love
and I am consumed with the desire to
love Thee and make Thee loved by all
men. The tears which well abundantly
in Thy sacred eyes appear

to me as so many precious pearls that I
love to gather up,
in order to purchase the souls of poor
sinners by means of
their infinite value. O Jesus, whose
adorable Face ravishes
my heart, I implore Thee to fix deep
within me
Thy divine image and to set me on fire
with Thy Love,
that I may be found worthy to come to
the contemplation
of Thy glorious Face in Heaven.

Canticle to the Holy Face

Jesus, Your ineffable image
is the star which guides my steps.
Ah, You know, Your sweet Face
Is for me Heaven on earth.
My love discovers the charms
Of Your Face adorned with tears.
I smile through my own tears
When I contemplate Your sorrows.

Oh! To console You I want
To live unknown on earth!
Your beauty, which You know how to veil,
Discloses for me all its mystery.
I would like to fly away to You!
Your Face is my only homeland.
It's my Kingdom of love.
It's my cheerful meadow.
Each day, my sweet sun.
It's the Lily of the Valley
Whose mysterious perfume
Consoles my exiled soul,
Making it taste the peace of Heaven.
It's my Rest, my Sweetness
And my melodious Lyre
Your Face, O my Sweet Savior,
Is the Divine Bouquet of Myrrh
I want to keep on my heart!
Your Face is my only wealth.
I ask for nothing more.
Hiding myself in it unceasingly,
I will resemble You, Jesus
Leave in me, the Divine Impress
Of Your features filled with sweetness,

And soon I'll become holy.
I shall draw hearts to You.
So that I may gather
A beautiful golden harvest,
Deign to set me aflame with Your Fire.
With Your adorned mouth,
Give me soon the Eternal Kiss!

13. Healing Scriptures

The Scriptures are full of passages that are meant to strengthen us through our sufferings. The following are healing scriptures taken from the New Testament of the Bible.

Matthew 8:16-17

When the even was come, they brought unto him many that were possessed with devils: and he cast out the spirits with his word, and healed all that were sick: That it might be fulfilled which was spoken by Esaias the prophet, saying, Himself took our infirmities, and bare our sicknesses.

Matthew 9:35

And Jesus went about all the cities and villages, teaching in their synagogues, and preaching the gospel of the kingdom, and healing every sickness and every disease among the people.

Matthew 15:30-31

And great multitudes came unto him, having with them those that were lame, blind, dumb, maimed, and many others, and cast them down at Jesus' feet; and he healed them: Insomuch that the multitude wondered, when they saw the dumb to speak, the maimed to be whole, the lame to walk, and the blind to see: and they glorified the God of Israel.

Mark 11:22-24

And Jesus answering saith unto them, Have faith in God. For verily I say unto you, that whosoever shall say unto this mountain, be thou removed, and be thou cast into the sea; and shall not doubt in his heart, but shall believe that those things which he saith shall come to pass; he shall have whatsoever he saith. Therefore I say unto you, What things so ever ye desire, when ye pray, believe that ye receive them, and ye shall have them.

Mark 16:17-18

And these signs shall follow them that believe; in my name shall they cast out devils; they shall speak with new tongues; they shall take up serpents; and if they drink any deadly thing, it shall not hurt them; they shall lay hands on the sick, and they shall recover.

Luke 4:17-19

And there was delivered unto him the book of the prophet Esaias. And when he had opened the book, he found the place where it was written, the Spirit of the Lord is upon me, because he hath anointed me to preach the gospel to the poor; he hath sent me to heal the brokenhearted, to preach deliverance to the captives, and recovering of sight to the blind, to set at liberty them that are bruised, to preach the acceptable year of the Lord.

Luke 9:1-2

Then he called his twelve disciples together, and gave them power and authority over all devils, and to cure diseases. And he sent them to preach the kingdom of God, and to heal the sick.

Acts 4:29-30

And now, Lord, behold their threatenings: and grant unto thy servants, that with all boldness they may speak thy word, by stretching forth thine hand to heal; and that signs and wonders may be done by the name of thy holy child Jesus.

Acts 10:38

How God anointed Jesus of Nazareth with the Holy Ghost and with power: who went about doing good and healing all that were oppressed of the devil; for God was with him.

James 5:13-16

Is any among you afflicted? Let him pray. Is any merry? Let him sing psalms. Is any sick among you? Let him call for the elders of the church; and let them pray over him, anointing him with oil in the name of the Lord: And the prayer of faith shall save the sick, and the Lord shall raise him up; and if he have committed sins, they shall be forgiven him. Confess your faults one to another, and pray one for another, that ye may be healed. The effectual fervent prayer of a righteous man availeth much.

1 John 5:14-15

And this is the confidence that we have in him, that if we ask any thing according to his will, he heareth us: And if we know that he hear us, whatsoever we ask, we know that we have the petitions that we desired of him.

14. Holy Face Picture

I hope that you will be thoroughly blessed and healed as you begin to venerate the Holy Face of Jesus and to offer it up to the Eternal Father for your

healing and blessings. Jesus is waiting for you to use the power that resides in his Holy Face. He has shown us His face and we are saved! He has shown us His face and we will be healed!
Amen

If you enjoyed this book, please tell others about it by leaving us a review on its Amazon page. Let us spread the devotion to the Holy Face of Jesus.

Holy Face Pictures Available at shop.thecatholicwomansvoice.com

Select Holy Face Images from the website menu.

Canvas Gallery Wrap or Framed Version Available.

Follow me on social media
@thecatholicwomansvoice
on YouTube and Instagram

Printed in Great Britain
by Amazon